D1123483

THE MILITARY EXPERIENCE.

Special Operations:
PARATROOPERS

THE MILITARY EXPERIENCE

Special Operations:
PARATROOPERS

DON NARDO

MORGAN REYNOLDS
PUBLISHING

GREENSBORO, NORTH CAROLINA

The Military Experience.
Special Operations: Paratroopers
Copyright © 2013 by Morgan Reynolds Publishing

Library of Congress Cataloging-in-Publication Data

Nardo, Don, 1947-
 Special operations : paratroopers / by Don Nardo.
    p. cm. -- (The military experience)
 Includes bibliographical references.
 ISBN 978-1-59935-360-9 -- ISBN 978-1-59935-361-6 (e-book) 1.
United
States--Armed Forces--Parachute troops. 2. United States--Armed
Forces--Commando troops. 3. Special forces (Military
science)--United
States. I. Title.
 UD483.N37 2013
 356'.1660973--dc23

                        2012019107

Printed in the United States of America
First Edition

Book cover and interior designed by:
Ed Morgan, navyblue design studio
Greensboro, NC

Table of Contents

Members from the 320th Special Tactics Squadron free fall after jumping from the back of a 1st Special Operations Squadron MC-130H Combat Talon II.

CHAPTER ONE

A KEY TOOL for Commandos

Drop zone controllers head out to recover a jumper from the 320th Special Tactics Squadron during Exercise Teak Torch in Udon Thani, Thailand.

It was still dark out in the early morning hours of December 20, 1989. The Panamanian soldiers guarding Rio Hato airfield, sixty-five miles from Panama City, quietly sat or strolled around. They were completely unaware of the danger that was rapidly approaching them. High above, a squadron of U.S. AC-130 gunships zeroed in on the airfield. Inside each plane were dozens of American commandos, or "special ops" warriors. Special ops is short for Special Operations Forces (SOF). The various kinds of fighters in the U.S. SOF carry out missions that are too difficult for ordinary soldiers.

An air-to-air view of a United States Air Force
AC-130 Hercules aircraft during target practice

UP AND DOWN THE RUNWAYS

At a given signal, the commandos began jumping from their planes. Plunging down through the inky darkness, they could see the airport's lights glowing below. As those beacons loomed closer, the men pulled their ripcords. That caused their parachutes to burst open and quickly slow their descent. Each was highly skilled in the art of parachuting. And together they belonged to the proud ranks of modern military parachute jumpers, most often called paratroopers.

These particular paratroopers were on a special mission. Their job was to spearhead the U.S. invasion of the small Central American nation of Panama. American leaders sought to depose a local military dictator and restore democracy there.

Many of the commandos assaulted the country's two main airfields. At Rio Hato, the first special ops men to reach the ground were Air Force Combat Controllers, or CCTs. Their dangerous task was to prepare the area for the rest of the commandos. The CCTs silently and efficiently set up control points from which to guide the incoming American planes and fighters.

Next came the Army Rangers and Air Force Pararescuemen, or PJs. The Rangers began to seize the airfield from the Panamanian guards. This ignited several gun battles, called firefights. Meanwhile, the PJs wound their way through the sprays of deadly bullets. Their job was to rescue and treat wounded Rangers, sometimes fighting enemy soldiers at the same time. "Speeding up and down the runway," one expert observer wrote, "the PJs collected the casualties and brought them to a collection point." There, they "provided the necessary medical attention until . . . evacuation could be arranged. All this time, firefights were going on around them."

DEVELOPMENT OF THE PARACHUTE

Rio Hato and the other airfield swiftly fell into U.S. hands, and the invasion of Panama was a success. Overall, members of several different U.S. special ops groups had taken part in the invasion. In addition to the Rangers, CCTs, and PJs, these included the Army's Special Forces, sometimes called the Green Berets. There were also a number of Navy SEALs involved. Whatever their units, most of the commandos who led the way in Panama parachuted in. In fact, the parachute is a key tool for modern special ops fighters. All American commandos are trained in parachute jumping, which plays a role in many of their missions.

They and other paratroopers owe much to the parachute's inventor, French scientist Louis-Sébastien Lenormand. His goal was to create a way for a person to safely escape from a damaged hot air balloon. In 1783, he personally tested his parachute, making it to the ground uninjured.

The first public parachute jump by Louis-Sébastien Lenormand in Montpellier, France, on December 26, 1783

SÉBASTIEN LENORMAND FAIT LA 1ʳᵉ EXPÉRIENCE DU PARACHUTE
MONTPELLIER (1783)

The application of the parachute to military operations emerged soon after the invention of airplanes in the early 1900s. In the 1920s, farsighted U.S. general Billy Mitchell recognized the potential of parachutes for pilots. He staged a demonstration at Kelly Airfield, in Texas. Six soldiers jumped from a plane and parachuted safely to the ground.

The military parachute really came of age during World War II (1939-1945). The Germans led the way. At the start of the conflict they outfitted all their pilots and many soldiers with chutes. The Americans and other Allies quickly caught up, however. Paratroopers were used to great effect in the Allied invasion of France in the closing months of the war.

A 1922 photo of a man parachuting

fact BOX

"Geronimo!"

One day during World War II, an American paratrooper named Aubrey Eberhart yelled "Geronimo!" as he jumped from his plane to show that he was as fearless as the Apache chief, Geronimo. After that, it became a tradition for U.S. paratroopers to scream that word while leaping out into the airy void.

An 1898 photo of Geronimo, leader of the Chiricahua Apache

"ELITE SHOCK TROOPERS"

As units of modern commandos began to form after World War II, they all adopted the parachute. It has proven essential in a wide variety of missions. Some, as in Panama in 1989, involve direct assaults on ground targets. Other missions require special ops warriors to parachute into hostile regions to set up secret observation bases.

Modern commandos also use parachutes when saving pilots whose planes have gone down behind enemy lines.

Often the only way the rescuers can get to the crash sites is to parachute in. Still another use of parachutes is to help free hostages held by enemies or criminals. A SEAL team parachuted into a pirate camp in Somalia early in 2012, for instance. The commandos rescued two kidnapped aid workers and killed all the pirates, all in a matter of minutes.

Clearly, the parachute has become an invaluable tool for the members of America's elite military forces. These men have become outstanding examples of the fighter described in an ode that honors all paratroopers. It is called the Parachutist's Creed. "A parachutist is not merely a soldier who arrives by parachute to fight," it says. Rather, he "is an elite shock trooper [who] his country expects . . . to march farther and faster, to fight harder, and to be more self-reliant than any other soldier."

the Paratroopers' Granddaddy

American commandos who become master parachute jumpers look back with pride on the paratroopers who preceded them. The primary forerunner, or granddaddy, of all modern U.S. paratroop units was the Army's 501st Parachute Infantry Regiment. It was created in November 1942 and was initially based at Camp Toccoa, Georgia. The group's first members were trained by legendary Army commander Colonel Howard "Skeets" Johnson. At the height of World War II, they flew to England. In June 1944, they jumped behind German lines in France. That made them the first Allied fighters to engage the enemy in the pivotal D-Day invasion.

501st Parachute Infantry Regiment Distinctive Unit Insignia

GERONIMO

CHAPTER TWO

The RIGORS of JUMP School

U.S. Air Force Senior Airman Travian Fearrington, a cross-training candidate for the combat controller career field, proceeds through the Special Tactics Obstacle Course at Hurlburt Field, Florida.

U.S. Army students from the Airborne School at Fort Benning, Georgia, are inspected by their jump masters prior to their first air-drop mission.

For modern American paratroopers, everything begins with "Jump School." That's the nickname for the U.S. Army Airborne School at Fort Benning, Georgia. All of the nation's commandos attend Jump School at one time or another. Among them are the Army's Rangers, Green Berets, and Delta Force; the Marines' Recon units; the Navy's SEALs and Special Boat units; and the Air Force's CCTs and PJs.

The parachute-jumping course these and other paratroopers take at Fort Benning lasts three weeks. All of those who have experienced it agree on one thing: The course is physically grueling and exhausting but well worth the time and effort. Those who graduate possess vital skills that benefit both them and their country.

LEARNING TO LAND

One reason that Jump School is so exhausting is that the various parachute-jumping exercises and drills are physically difficult. Added to that is the fact that performing them well and safely demands a good deal of physical conditioning. So in addition to learning to jump, the recruits do exercises similar to those in military boot camp. These include push-ups, sit-ups, and lots of running. The late Army paratrooper Kurt Gabel described the punishing early morning runs he endured during his own parachute course in the 1940s:

> Dawn was breaking. Sweat was running into my eyes and my aching legs grew weak and rubbery. Worst of all, I had lost control of my breath. It was now coming fast and wheezing through my wide-open mouth. . . . How far had we come? How much farther? "Hut-two-three-four," [the drill master droned over and over]. An ambulance, following the battalion like a vulture, would pick up the ones who had fainted. Lucky guys.

The rigors of Jump School are divided into three phases, each a week long. The first is called "Ground Week." During this period the recruits learn to land safely on the ground. It is true that a parachute significantly slows a jumper's downward speed. Yet he or she still hits the ground with considerable force. Many jumpers have been badly injured, or even killed, because they landed the wrong way. The recruits start by jumping from platforms only a few feet high. Day-by-day, however, the platforms get higher.

The second phase, "Tower Week," is so named because the platforms the recruits must jump from are towers. Each person wears a suspension harness that slows their rate of fall. So when they jump from a tower they get a partial feeling for what a real jump will be like. One tower is 34 feet (10.3 m) high. Another is a whopping 250 feet (76 m) tall. Also during Tower Week, the trainees learn how to line up inside a plane in preparation for a jump. When the "jumpmaster" orders someone to jump, he or she must do it without hesitation.

Paratroopers performing a practice jump in 1951 during the Korean War

fact BOX

Earning Badges

Graduates of the paratrooper course at the U.S. Army Airborne School at Fort Benning are eligible for a special insignia. It is called the Parachutist Badge, sometimes called the "Jump Wings." Graduates who go on to do at least thirty jumps can qualify for the Senior Parachutist Badge.

U.S. Army Airborne
Basic Parachutist Badge

Airmen from the 346th and 342nd Training Squadrons perform a high-altitude, low-opening parachute jump onto the parade grounds at Lackland Air Force Base in San Antonio, Texas.

THAT BEAUTIFUL EXPANSE OF NYLON

Finally comes the third phase of training—"Jump Week." As the name suggests, the recruits perform actual parachute jumps. Here, all their former training and conditioning comes into play. They must do five jumps, one of them at night, in order to graduate. Gabel left behind this vivid memory of his first jump:

> My hands pushed away from the bulk-heads and my left leg propelled my body out. . . . My eyes were open, just as I had been taught, and my head was down. . . . There was no sensation of falling. It was rather as if a huge wave had caught me and was pushing me down. [When I pulled the cord] I was jarred to what felt like a dead stop. My arms went up [and] I managed to squeeze my head back to look at the canopy above. There it was—white, beautiful, and *open* . . . that beautiful expanse of nylon!

Upon finishing Jump School, the graduates are full-fledged paratroopers. The commandos among them go their separate ways. Some of them end up using what they learned often. Others do so only on occasion. Either way, they become part of what an Army spokesperson calls "an elite body of fighting men and women—people who have always set the example for determination and courage." When they seek and receive paratrooper training, he says, they "accept the challenge of continuing this tradition."

A HELLUVA Way to Die

Over the years, U.S. paratroopers attending Jump School adopted a comical song titled "Blood on the Risers." They sing it to the tune of the "Battle Hymn of the Republic." Its several verses, including the one that follows, joke about parachute jumpers who made mistakes and died as a result.

He counted long, he counted loud, he waited for the shock,
He felt the wind, he felt the cold, he felt the awful drop,
The silk from his reserve spilled out and wrapped around his legs,
And he ain't gonna jump no more.
 (CHORUS)
Gory, gory, what a helluva way to die,
Gory, gory, what a helluva way to die,
Gory, gory, what a helluva way to die,
He ain't gonna jump no more!

A paratrooper with a T-10D parachute prepares to land at Holland Drop Zone at Fort Bragg, North Carolina. The T-10 series of parachutes have been in service with the Army since the 1950s.

CHAPTER THREE

Like TAXI CABS in the Sky

An AC-130U gunship from the 4th Special Operations Squadron. The AC-130 gunship's primary missions are close air support, air interdiction, and force protection.

Paratroopers from the 82nd Airborne Division board a C-130 Hercules aircraft for Haiti after an earthquake hit the Caribbean nation in 2010 .

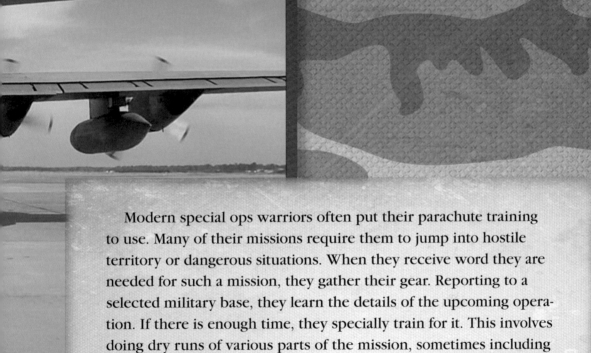

Modern special ops warriors often put their parachute training to use. Many of their missions require them to jump into hostile territory or dangerous situations. When they receive word they are needed for such a mission, they gather their gear. Reporting to a selected military base, they learn the details of the upcoming operation. If there is enough time, they specially train for it. This involves doing dry runs of various parts of the mission, sometimes including practice jumps.

When it is time to perform the actual mission, the commandos board their transport. These planes are a lot like taxi cabs in the sky. They pick up their passengers, take them to a preplanned location, and let them out. That location is the jump point. Leaping from the plane, the commandos execute the specific kind of jump called for in the mission. Several different kinds exist. And the leaders of the operation choose the one that offers the best chance of success.

THE MOST POPULAR TRANSPORT

The transports that ferry the special ops fighters to the jump point are specially constructed for the job. The most versatile and popular of these planes is the C-130 Hercules transport. First introduced in the 1950s, many different versions of it have been designed over the years.

The newest versions of the plane feature the latest radar, tracking devices, and other advanced onboard systems. According to one military observer, the C-130's "sensor package includes television [and] infrared and radar components, which allow the aircraft to identify targets and friendly forces any time, any place. . . . Navigational devices include inertial navigation and global positioning systems [GPS]."

These GPS devices use data produced by numerous orbiting satellites. They allow the pilot to pinpoint a target destination anywhere in the world with amazing accuracy. One Navy SEAL who parachuted from a C-130 later said, "I can't say enough about our special operations pilots. They made a straight pass in and dropped us right onto the insertion point." The latest C-130s also have instruments that can jam, or block, enemy communications. That means that these planes can often fly in and out of enemy-controlled areas without being detected.

In addition, the C-130 carries powerful machine guns, missiles, and other weapons systems. These sometimes provide support to commandos who have already jumped and reached the ground. If large groups of enemy fighters attack the commandos, the C-130 can swoop down. Flying low, it can open fire and devastate the attackers.

SPECIAL OPERATIONS: PARATROOPERS

Soldiers from the 82nd Airborne Division are being picked up so they can jump to earn foreign "Jump Wings" during Operation Toy Drop. Operation Toy Drop is an annual jump hosted by the U.S. Army Civil Affairs and Psychological Operations Command (Airborne) and supported by Fort Bragg's XVIII Airborne Corps and Pope Air Force Base's 43rd Airlift Wing. Operation Toy Drop gives soldiers and airmen the opportunity to help local families in need while boosting morale and incorporating valuable training.

A member of the high-altitude, low-opening or HALO team jumps at 12,500 feet.

A RANGE OF JUMPS

In fact, this ability to fly low is one of the reasons special ops fighters like the C-130 so much. Another expert observer said these planes are popular with commandos because "they can fly low, slow, and long distances." For example, moving slowly at a low altitude is perfect for one of the jumps the commandos perform often. Called the HALO jump, its goal is to get them to the ground fast and make it hard for the enemy to see them. The letters stand for "High-Altitude, Low-Opening." As these words suggest, the jumper exits the plane at a high altitude. Most commonly it is 32,000 feet (10,000 m) and directly above the target. The paratrooper plummets downward rapidly. He opens his chute only after reaching 2,500 feet (760 m).

In contrast, at times the commandos don't want to risk the C-130 being detected by enemy radar. So they employ a jump called the HAHO, or "High-Altitude, High-Opening." In it, they leave the plane when it is dozens of miles from the target, far from radar devices. As in the HALO jump, they start out at 32,000 feet. But in this case, the commandos open their chutes after a mere nine or ten seconds. As the transport veers away, they begin descending. Slowly but steadily they drift toward the target. Their ability to accomplish this and a range of other jumps significantly increases the odds that their mission will be successful.

JUMPING in Formation

Often in HAHO jumps performed at night, commandos jump in formation, or together. They leave the plane at the same time and remain linked until shortly before deploying their chutes. This is done to ensure that each sees what the others are doing. That way their chutes cannot accidentally become tangled. Noted PJ Jack Brehm describes such a formation:

> The team has formed a circle about thirty feet across. Each jumper faces toward the center of the circle so that they can keep an eye on one another. They'll hold this formation until they reach 6,000 feet, at which point they'll break off. . . . At 5,000 feet, each jumper begins his pull sequence, first looking over his shoulder to make sure the air is clear above him.

fact BOX

The C-130's Full Capacity

The C-130 Hercules transport often carries a small group of commandos to a jump point. But the plane's full capacity is much larger. It can fit as many as sixty-four paratroopers equipped with their chutes, survival gear, and an array of rifles and other weapons.

Air Force special operations command airmen load onto an MC-130P Combat Shadow before departing for Haiti on January 13, 2010, as part of the U.S. humanitarian assistance and disaster relief mission following a catastrophic earthquake.

60217

CHAPTER FOUR

So That OTHERS May LIVE

A mass airborne operation involving more than 1,000 soldiers of the 75th Ranger Regiment begins the biennial Ranger Rendezvous at Fort Benning, Georgia.

All U.S. commandos have used their parachutes at one time or another. But none have done so as often as those in the Air Force Special Operations Command (AFSOC). Its special ops fighters are the Pararescuemen, or PJs, and the Combat Control Teams, or CCTs.

The PJs, short for "Pararescue Jumpers," have one of the toughest jobs in the entire U.S. military. They rescue fellow military personnel, and civilians too, under the harshest, most dangerous conditions. Their training is far-reaching and intense. They must be skilled at far more than just parachuting. The PJs are also expert medical technicians, swimmers, scuba divers, mountaineers, and survivalists.

In addition, the PJs are often called on to save and protect their patients while under enemy fire. So these commandos also receive weapons and combat training similar to that of the Army Rangers and Navy SEALs. Thus, although the PJs are trained to save lives, on occasion they must take some as well. As veteran PJ Craig Guthridge said:

> We're not about death and destruction, and blowing stuff up. We want to get in and get out . . . no fuss, no muss. But we're not going to raise the white flag the first time the enemy says "boo!" either. We're just as skilled in taking lives as we are at saving them. And sometimes you have to do bad stuff to get the good guy out.

A pararescueman provides medical attention to an Afghan who has suffered gunshot injuries.

fact BOX

Valiant Efforts

During the U.S. wars in Iraq and Afghanistan alone, the valiant efforts of the Air Force Pararescuemen saved the lives of more than 750 people.

PJs perform hoist extraction of a survivor during an urban operations training exercise in Iraq.

The PJs are therefore extremely versatile, or flexible and adaptable. They are willing to do anything, even to risk their lives, to save others. This selfless attitude inspired their famous motto, "That others may live."

THE PIPELINE

The formation of a group of rescuers who would later become the PJs occurred during World War II. At first, the group was called the Air Rescue Service. In 1956, the military changed its name to the Air Rescue and Recovery Service. Eventually, it received the title USAF Pararescue.

The military also instituted special schooling for the group's multitalented members. Called the "Pipeline," it lasts two years. The recruits spend time at various bases across the country, where they endure often grueling training programs. Some idea of the difficulty of the training comes from remarks made by one of the scuba instructors. "We want to break the students down, crack them open, and peek inside them to see what they're made of," he said and added:

> We want to find out how they'll react after missing 24 hours of sleep, when they're totally spent, sore and hungry. . . . We want to find out if they're quitters. Without drive and determination, you'll fail the mission. If you fail in the pool, no problem, we'll drag you out and send you home. But fail on a mission and you come home in a body bag. Maybe your whole team comes home in body bags.

A GRATEFUL HUMANITY

Such rigorous training has paid off. The modern PJs are commandos of the highest caliber. About 450 of them are on active duty at any given time. Since the infamous 9/11 attacks in 2001, they have carried out more than 12,000 combat rescue missions. Many of these heroic actions required the PJs to execute daring parachute jumps.

One such mission took place on March 12, 2012, about 700 miles (1,127 km) off the coast of Acapulco, Mexico. Two men aboard a Chinese fishing vessel had been badly burned in a diesel fire. The boat did not have the medical personnel or equipment needed to save them. So the captain sent out a distress call.

Answering that call, the nearest PJs, in San Diego, California, swung into action. They loaded rescue equipment into two C-130s and two helicopters and headed out to sea. The faster C-130s reached the fishing vessel first. As they circled above, four PJs parachuted from them and splashed down into the ocean near the boat. They quickly boarded the vessel and removed an array of medical supplies from their packs.

While treating the burned fishermen, the PJs consulted with doctors via radio. The doctors recommended that the patients be taken to a burn treatment center in San Diego. By this time, the helicopters had arrived. They picked up the patients and PJs and rushed them to San Diego. Soon afterward, the local PJs' commander, Colonel Steven J. Butow, said, "I could not be prouder of our airmens' extraordinary efforts during this mission." He added that the rescue was "a testament" to the vital services the PJs provide "the nation" and a grateful humanity.

One of two pararescuemen from the 38th Rescue Squadron follows an inflatable boat out the back of an HC-130 during a rescue mission 350 miles northeast of the Caribbean island of St. Maarten. They provided medical support to a Chinese fisherman who sustained a life-threatening chest injury the day before.

The rescue of some plane crash victims during World War II along the China-Burma border (*circled on the map*) inspired the formation of a group of rescuers that later became the Air Force's Pararescue Jumpers.

Birth of the PJs

The roots of the Air Force Pararescuemen stretch back to World War II. At the time, the Allies—the United States and its partner nations—were fighting the Japanese Empire. In 1943, an Allied plane carrying twenty-one people crashed near the China-Burma border in southern Asia. Several of the survivors were badly injured. The area where the plane went down was very remote, with no roads leading in. It was also crawling with Japanese soldiers. The only way to save the crash victims was for a team to parachute in. Its members would obviously need military as well as medical skills. A handful of U.S. soldiers volunteered to parachute into the crash site. In a heroic effort, they managed to save the victims and bring them home. This marked the birth of the group that later became the PJs.

CHAPTER FIVE

The Air Force's PATHFINDERS

A U.S. Air Force combat controller signals to other controllers and U.S. Army pathfinders at a drop zone survey outside Port-au-Prince, Haiti, during Operation Unified Response on January 24, 2010.

The PJs' job—to rescue people under difficult conditions—is easy for everyone to understand. The average person readily visualizes them parachuting from planes, landing in the midst of turmoil, and saving lives. But this is not the case with the Air Force Special Operations Command's other commando group. The Combat Control Technicians (or Teams), called CCTs for short, are also paratroopers who perform dangerous missions. However, they have a serious image problem. Put simply, they are the least understood of all U.S. special ops units.

"Most Americans aren't aware of what we do," said CCT paratrooper Paul "Vinnie" Venturella. "And much of what we do isn't very sexy. We don't have movies made about us," like the Navy SEALs and Army Green Berets do. Another CCT, James "Ski" Pulaski, agreed. "No one really understands [what we do]," he remarked with a smile. "They think we control combat. Even my wife has a hard time explaining what I do, so she tells people I'm a cook!"

U.S. Air Force combat controllers and U.S. Army pathfinders conduct a drop zone survey outside Port-au-Prince, Haiti.

FIRST ON THE SCENE

Venturella tried to explain the CCTs' main mission using three words, "shoot, move, communicate." What he means is that the CCTs first parachute, unseen, into hostile situations. Usually they land in war zones filled with enemy soldiers. So once they're on the ground, they must sometimes shoot and kill one or more of those soldiers. Then, when possible, the CCTs move to a place where they can be alone and hidden. It can be an abandoned house, a cave, or a wooded grove. Or sometimes it is a small hut the paratroopers throw together themselves.

In these spots, the CCTs set up makeshift communications stations. Using them, they take on the roles of spies and air traffic controllers. With their advanced radio equipment, they tell U.S. forces what is happening in the target area. They also direct American helicopters and planes to safe places to land. At the same time, they warn those aircraft to avoid *unsafe* places. In a way, the CCTs are pathfinders for the Air Force and other military branches.

The CCTs perform these and other highly hazardous jobs alone, virtually without help or support. This is because they are the first U.S. fighters on the scene in a particular combat zone. Therefore, their motto, "First There," is very fitting. In the words of an unnamed Air Force officer, it "reaffirms the combat controller's commitment to undertaking the most dangerous missions behind enemy lines by leading the way for other forces to follow."

To successfully carry out their nearly superhuman tasks, CCTs must undergo enormous amounts of training. In bases across the United States, they learn to parachute, scuba dive, and operate small boats and all sorts of land vehicles. They also become adept in survival methods, mountain climbing, and rappelling down ropes. In addition, CCTs are experts in land navigation, electronic equipment, communications, sniper rifles, and explosives.

The Pathfinder Badge

fact BOX

The Original CCTs

The Air Force combat controllers originated during World War II. At that time they were part of the Army and called "pathfinders." They entered combat areas before the main assault forces and provided weather and navigation information for those forces.

A combat controller during a simulated patrol in a military operation in an urban terrain exercise

AN EXTREMELY RISKY JUMP

The combat controllers' skills have often been tested in battle. One memorable incident occurred in October 1983. The U.S. military invaded the small Caribbean island-nation of Grenada. Between 1979 and 1983, a Communist-inspired coup had taken place there. The democratic government had fallen. And the U.S. invasion—dubbed Operation Urgent Fury—aimed to restore that democracy.

In the opening hours of the invasion, a squadron of C-130s approached the island's main airfield. Several combat controllers executed an extremely hard and risky parachute jump. Carrying heavy loads of supplies, they leapt from the planes at a height of only 500 feet (153 m). If they failed to open their chutes immediately, they would likely not survive the fall.

All of the CCTs reached the ground safely. Wasting no time, they cleared the runway of numerous trucks and cars parked there. All the while, they dodged swarms of bullets from the local guards. Next, the CCTs, aided by a few Army Rangers, fought their way into and seized the control tower. From there, they directed the safe landing of American planes and helicopters.

In the years since Urgent Fury, the CCTs have remained "First There" in many U.S. military operations. Other paratroopers often follow them into the fray. Frequently they include PJs, Rangers, Green Berets, and/or SEALs. In this way, when the situation demands it, America's daring special ops warriors first master the air. Then they take control of the land and sea, almost always assuring the mission's ultimate success.

U.S. Air Force combat controllers and U.S. Army pathfinders survey an area as a possible drop zone outside Port-au-Prince, Haiti, during Operation Unified Response.

Having the "JUICE"

Clearly, no human could accomplish the many hard, often death-defying jobs the CCTs do without being in good shape. So all combat controllers work out in the gym regularly. "The nature of the business requires [that] these guys have the 'juice' it takes to be in top physical condition," says Air Force lieutenant Carie A. Seydel. The Air Force wants to ensure that no one slacks off in this intense physical training. So it tests the CCTs at least once a year. They have to run 3 miles (4.8 km) and swim 4,920 feet (1,500 m). They must also do large numbers of push-ups, sit-ups, and pull-ups in an allotted time.

Combat controllers practice firing movements on the range at a forward-deployed location supporting Operation Enduring Freedom.

Source Notes

Chapter 1: A Key Tool for Commandos

p. 12,   "Speeding up and down . . ." Fred Pushies, *Deadly Blue: Battle Stories of the U.S. Air Force Special Operations Command* (New York: AMACOM, 2009), 12.

p. 16,   "A parachutist is . . ." Bob Konings, "The Story of Jo Chicchinelli," http://www.joecicchinelli.com/Misc Poems.htm.

Chapter 2: The Rigors of Jump School

p. 21,   "Dawn was breaking," Kurt Gabel, *The Making of a Paratrooper: Airborne Training and Combat in World War II* (Lawrence, KS: University Press of Kansas, 1990), 51.

p. 25,   "My hands pushed away . . ." Ibid., 116-117.

p. 25,   "an elite body . . ." U.S. Army, "Soldier Life: Airborne School," http://www.goarmy.com/soldier-life/being-a-soldier/ongoing-training/specialized-schools/airborne-school.html http://www.goarmy.com/soldier-life/being-a-soldier/ongoing-training/specialized-schools/airborne-school.html http://www.goarmy.com/soldier-life/being-a-soldier/ongoing-training/specialized-schools/airborne-school.html http://www.goarmy.com/soldier-life/being-a-soldier/ongoing-training/specialized-schools/airborne-school.html.

p. 26,   "He counted long . . ." 101st Airborne Division, "Blood on the Risers," http://www.menofeasycompany.com/home/index.php?page_id=152.

Chapter 3: Like Taxi Cabs in the Sky

p. 32,   "sensor package includes . . ." Harold Kennedy, "Why Special Ops Prefer C-130s for Many Missions," http://www.nationaldefensemagazine.org/archive/2002/february/pages/why_special_ops4142.aspx.

p. 32,   "I can't say enough . . ." Dick Couch, *Down Range: Navy SEALs in the War on Terrorism* (New York: Three Rivers Press, 2005), 77.

p. 35,   "they can fly low . . ." Kennedy, "Why Special Ops Prefer C-130s for Many Missions."

p. 36,   "The team has formed . . ." Jack Brehm and Pete Nelson, *That Others May Live: The True Story of the PJs* (New York: Three Rivers Press, 2001), 7.

Chapter 4: So That Others May Live

p. 40,   "We're not about death . . ." Master Sgt. Pat McKenna, "Superman School," http://www.militaryspot.com/career/featured_military_jobs/.

p. 43,   "That others way live," Department of the Air Force, "Pararescue History," http://www.pararescue.com/history.aspx?id=449.

p. 43,   "We want to find out . . ." McKenna, "Superman School."

p. 44,   "I could not be prouder. . ." Donald G. LeBlanc, "Complex Pararescue Mission Saves Fishermen Off Mexico Coast," http://www.af.mil/news/story.asp?id=123293604 http://www.af.mil/news/story.asp?id=123293604.

Chapter 5: The Air Force's Pathfinders

p. 50,   "Most Americans aren't aware . . ." Carie A. Seydel, "Air Force Combat Controllers: Shoot, Move, Communicate," http://usmilitary.about.com/od/airforce/l/blcct.htm http://usmilitary.about.com/od/airforce/l/blcct.htm http://usmilitary.about.com/od/airforce/l/blcct.htm.

p. 50,   "No one really understands . . ." Ibid.

p. 51,   "shoot, move . . ." Ibid.

p. 51,   "First There," U.S. Air Force, "Combat Controllers," http://www.af.mil/information/factsheets/factsheet.asp?id=174.

p. 51,   "reaffirms the combat controller's commitment . . ." Ibid.

p. 55,   "The nature of the business . . ." Seydel, "Air Force Combat Controllers."

Glossary

beret: A small cloth cap worn by members of the Army Special Forces.

CCT: Short for Combat Control Technician (or Team), a type of U.S. Air Force commando.

chute: The shortened version of parachute.

civilian: A person who is not in the armed forces.

commando: An elite, specially trained soldier who is assigned to difficult, dangerous missions; or a special ops fighter.

firefight: A battle involving firearms.

formation: Relating to parachuting, a group jump, when two or more people jump together.

Geronimo!: A word that many paratroopers yell as they leap from their plane; the word comes from the name of a famous Apache Indian leader.

HAHO ("High-altitude, High-opening"): a parachute jump in which the person leaves the plane high in the sky and opens the chute a few seconds later.

HALO ("High-altitude, Low-opening"): a parachute jump in which the person leaves the plane high in the sky and opens the chute not very far above the ground.

jumpmaster: In the military, a group leader who is in charge of the parachute jumpers on a plane and tells them when to jump.

paratrooper: A military parachute jumper.

PJ: Short for Pararescue Jumper, or Pararescueman, a type of U.S. Air Force commando.

police action: An attack or invasion made by one country against another to stop supposed crimes or other illegal activities.

regiment: A large group of soldiers.

rip cord: The string a parachute jumper pulls to release his or her parachute.

special ops: Short for Special Operations Forces (SOF), consisting of the U.S. military's elite units of soldiers; or commandos.

Bibliography

Brehm, Jack, and Pete Nelson. *That Others May Live: The True Story of the PJs.* New York: Three Rivers Press, 2001.

Carney, John T., Jr., and Benjamin F. Schemmer. *No Room for Error: The Covert Operations of America's Special Tactics Units from Iran to Afghanistan.* New York: Ballantine, 2002.

Cooke, Tim. *U.S. Army Special Forces.* New York: Powerkids Press, 2012.

Couch, Dick. *Chosen Soldier: The Making of a Special Forces Warrior.* New York: Three Rivers Press, 2008.

Gabel, Kurt. *The Making of a Paratrooper: Airborne Training and Combat in World War II.* Lawrence, KS: University Press of Kansas, 1990.

Jacobellis, Nick. "Pararescue Jumpers." http://www.tactical-life.com/online/tactical-weapons/pararescue-jumpers/.

Labrecque, Ellen. *Special Forces.* Mankrato, MN: Heinemann-Raintree, 2012.

Montana, Jack. *Parachute Regiment.* Broomall, PA: Mason Crest, 2011.

Nagle, Jeanne. *Delta Force.* New York: Gareth Stevens, 2012.

Nelson, Drew. *Green Berets.* New York: Gareth Stevens, 2012.

Pushies, Fred J. *Special Ops: America's Elite Forces in 21st Century Combat.* St. Paul: MBI, 2003.

Sandler, Micahel. *Pararescumen in Action.* New York: Bearport, 2008.

Sherwood, Ben. "Lessons in Survival: The Science that Explains Why Elite Military Forces Bounce Back Faster than the Rest of Us." http://www.thedailybeast.com/newsweek/2009/02/13/lessons-in-survival.html.

Web sites

Become a U.S. A.F. Combat Controller
http://usafcca.org/cca/careers/

Organizing for Search and Rescue
http://www.airpower.au.af.mil/airchronicles/apj/apj95/sum95_files/meggett.htm

Pararescue History
http://www.pararescue.com/history.aspx?id=449

U.S. Air Force. Fact Sheet for the AC-130 Spectre Gunship.
http://www.af.mil/information/factsheets/factsheet.asp?fsID=71

U.S. Air Force. Fact Sheet for the Weapons of the Special Forces.
http://www.af.mil/information/factsheets/factsheet.asp?fsID=3668

U.S.A.F. Pararescue. "Superman School."
http://www.pararescue.com/unitinfo.aspx?id=490

Index

Photo Credits

All images used in this book that are not in the public domain are credited in the listing that follows: